W9-AUJ-083

WITHDRAWN

THE ANCIENT WORLD

ANCIENT AZTECS

BY MICHAEL BURGAN

CHILDREN'S PRESS®
AN IMPRINT OF SCHOLASTIC INC.
NEW YORK TORONTO LONDON AUCKLAND SYDNEY
MEXICO CITY NEW DELHI HONG KONG
DANBURY, CONNECTICUT

Library of Congress Cataloging-in-Publication Data
Burgan, Michael.
  Ancient aztecs/by Michael Burgan.
    p. cm.—(The ancient world)
  Includes bibliographical references and index.
  ISBN: 978-0-531-25175-1 (lib. bdg.)
  ISBN: 978-0-531-25975-7 (pbk.)
  1. Aztecs—Juvenile literature. I. Title.
  F1219.73.B86 2012
  972—dc23   2012002437

Photographs © 2013: Alamy Images: 27 bottom (Chuck Place), 49 bottom (David A. Barnes), 66 bottom (Iain Masterton), 19, 102 top (Mary Evans Picture Library), 86 (The Art Gallery Collection), 27 top (WILDLIFE GmbH); AP Images: 45 (Charles Rex Arbogast), 96 (Nam Y. Huh), 42, 67, 80, 92 (North Wind Picture Archives); Bridgeman Art Library: 44 (Biblioteca Medicea-Laurenziana, Florence, Italy), 82 (Diego Duran/Biblioteca Nacional, Madrid, Spain/Giraudo), 6 (Diego Rivera/Palacio Nacional, Mexico City, Mexico/Bildarchiv Steffens Henri Stierlin), 70 (Musee de l'Homme, Paris, France), 83 top (Museo de America, Madrid, Spain), 11 (Museo del Templo Mayor, Mexico City, Mexico/Bildarchiv Steffens Henri Stierlin), 17 (Museo Nacional de Antropologia, Mexico City, Mexico/Ian Mursell/Mexicolore), 22 (Palazzo Pitti, Florence, Italy); Corbis Images: cover main (Kenneth Garrett/National Geographic Society), cover right inset, 1 (Sergio Dorantes); Dreamstime: 75 (Michal Adamczyk), 95 (Tomas Hes); Getty Images: 15 (DeAgostini), 29 (Diego Duran), 91 (Dorling Kindersley), 46 (Field Museum Library); iStockphoto/OGphoto: 14, 100 top; Landov/Jorge Rios Ponce/DPA: 62; Newscom: 77 (akg-images/Veintimilla), 69 (Oronoz), 21 (Prisma); Shutterstock, Inc.: page borders throughout (ChaosMakers), 83 bottom (Dmitriy Shironosov), 13 top (Globe Turner, LLC), 12, 100 bottom (Vadim Petrakov); Superstock, Inc.: 87, 103 (Bridgeman Art Library, London), 35 (Christian Kober/Robert Harding Picture Library), 4, 10, 18, 26, 36 top, 50, 55, 58, 65, 66 top, 74, 78, 101, 102 bottom (DeAgostini), 13 bottom, 63, 84, 89 (Image Asset Management, Ltd.), 36 bottom, 79 (National Geographic), 90 (Pantheon), 40 (Science and Society), 8, 24, 25, 32 (The Art Archive), 28 (Universal Images Group), 9, 68, 73, 81; The Art Archive/Picture Desk: 57 (Museo Ciudad Mexico/Collection Dagli Orti), 5, 31 (National Anthropological Museum Mexico/Gianni Dagli Orti), 47, 48 (Templo Mayor Library Mexico/Gianni Dagli Orti); The Granger Collection: cover left inset, back cover top, 3, 38, 53, 56, 61; The Image Works: 49 top (akg-images), 7 (J. Bedmar/Iberfoto), 39 (Roger-Viollet), 93 (Werner Forman/HIP).

Maps by XNR Productions, Inc.

Content Consultant: Susan Toby Evans, PhD, Professor of Anthropology, Pennsylvania State University, University Park, Pennsylvania

1 2 3 4 5 6 7 8 9 10 R 22 21 20 19 18 17 16 15 14 13

JOURNEY BACK TO THE ANCIENT AZTECS

Modern-day Mexico City is built upon the site of Tenochtitlan.

More than a million people still speak the Aztec language of Nahuatl.

Tenochtitlan was once home to as many as fifty thousand people.

TABLE OF CONTENTS

A statue from the ancient
city of Texcoco

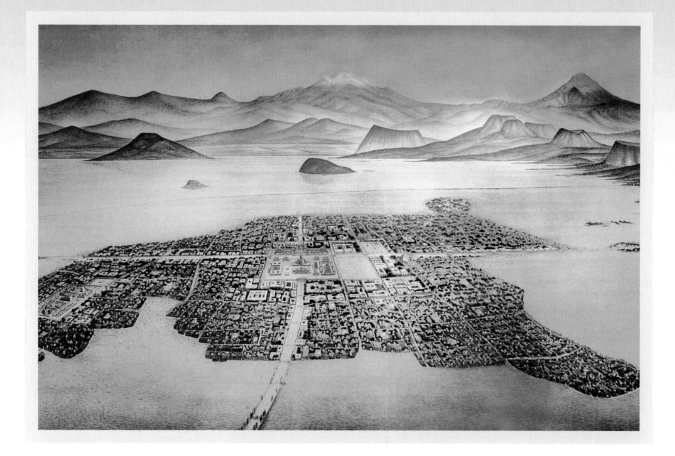

Several islands dotted the lakes, and one of them was the home of a great ancient city, Tenochtitlan. At its height during the early sixteenth century, as many as fifty thousand people lived there. It was the capital of the Aztec Empire.

The early history of the Mexica (pronounced meh-SHEE-kah), the people known today as the Aztecs, is cloudy. The Aztecs told myths to explain their journey from the north into the Valley of Mexico. But along with the myths are many truths, as documented in the records the Aztecs kept of their empire. Stories that passed from one generation to the next were later written down,

Tenochtitlan was built on islands in Lake Texcoco.

The Aztecs cultivated corn and other crops.

leaving behind a rich history of this Middle American civilization.

During their travels and upon their arrival in the Valley of Mexico, the Aztecs absorbed influences from the people around them. Then, in a quest for riches, they used their abilities as warriors to spread their domination over hundreds of miles.

Although skilled on the battlefield, the Aztecs were more than just soldiers. Their population included engineers, farmers, priests, merchants, and artists. They developed different schools to train their young and kept careful records of the **tribute** they collected from the peoples they ruled. Their rulers ate lavish meals in huge palaces, and the government held many festivals to honor the Aztecs' gods. The Aztecs believed these gods influenced all parts of human life, and religion was a key part of Aztec culture. The Aztecs believed the gods had chosen them for greatness. Yet they also believed that even their great civilization would end, as other worlds had ended before theirs.

tribute (TRIB-yoot) something done, given, or said to show thanks or respect, or to repay an obligation

The Aztec Empire began forming during the fourteenth century and was still growing in 1519. That year, soldiers from a distant nation reached Tenochtitlan. They were Spaniards, eager to claim land for Spain in a hunt for gold and other riches. The meeting of these two empires in the Valley of Mexico is one of the great events in world history. For the Aztecs, the arrival of the Spanish meant an end to their rule. But the Aztecs were not forgotten. In their later travels, the Spanish spread parts of Aztec culture around the world. The Aztecs built on the achievements of civilizations before them and then created their own with lasting influence.

The arrival of the Spanish marked the beginning of the end of the Aztec Empire.

CHAPTER ONE

A WANDERING TRIBE BUILDS AN EMPIRE

Starting in the twelfth century, tribes in present-day northern Mexico began to **migrate** south. Perhaps changes in climate made it hard for them to hunt or raise crops on their traditional lands—no one knows for sure. But whatever drove them to

According to legend, the Mexica traveled to the Valley of Mexico from a place called Aztlan.

This Aztec carving depicts the dismembered body of the goddess Coyolxauhqui.

seek a new home, these people eventually reached the Valley of Mexico. The last of these tribes to arrive was the Mexica.

The Mexica claimed that their homeland was an island in a lake called Aztlan, meaning "the place of the white heron." Aztlan was the source of the word *Aztec*, by which the world knows these people today. Leading the Mexica on their search for a new home was a warrior chief named Huitzilopochtli. After his death, he became a god, and he continued to speak to the Mexica through their priests. The people sometimes stayed in one location for up to twenty years, farming and erecting buildings. But Huitzilopochtli, the Mexica believed, always told them to move on. The priests told the people

migrate (MYE-grate) to move from one country or area to another

Many elaborate carvings decorate the ruins of Teotihuacan.

Mesoamerica (mez-oh-uh-MARE-in-kuh) the area extending from central Mexico south to Honduras and Nicaragua in which pre-Columbian cultures thrived

that the god had a plan for them. Huitzilopochtli was leading them to a spot where they would build the seat of their great empire—Tenochtitlan.

SETTLING IN THE VALLEY OF MEXICO

Historians today consider the story of Huitzilopochtli a myth. But no one disputes that the Mexica were a wandering people who settled in the Valley of Mexico. They were latecomers to **Mesoamerica**, arriving sometime between 1250 and 1300 CE.

The Mexica and the earlier migrants from the north found some residents who had adopted the urban culture of the great civilizations of the past. These earlier peoples included the unknown builders of Teotihuacan and the Toltecs. Teotihuacan was home to about 100,000 people at its peak of power, around 500 CE, making it one of the largest cities in the world. To the Aztecs, Teotihuacan was important because they believed their gods had met there to create the Fifth Sun—the current period of life on Earth. The name for the city came from Nahuatl words meaning "place of the gods." The Aztecs prized the art they found in the ruins of Teotihuacan.

The Past Is Present
THEIR NAMES LIVE ON

T he names of many places in today's world have their roots in words used by the Mexica and Aztecs. The country name *Mexico* is one example. The names are often combinations of words from Nahuatl, the language of the Mexica and their neigh- boring tribes. *Metepec*, the name of a city in south-central Mexico, means "in the mountain of maguey plants." Metepec was one of many towns mentioned on a sixteenth-century painted document called the *Codex Mendoza* (left). It was created by

an Aztec artist for the Spaniards and is still used by historians today to understand the Aztec world. The names of numerous ani- mals, plants, fruits, vegetables, and beverages we use today also come from Nahuatl. For example, the word *chocolate* comes from the Nahuatl word *chocolatl*, and the word avo- cado comes from the Nahuatl word *ahuacatl*. *Chicle*, the Spanish word for chewing gum, comes from the Nahuatl word *tziktli*. Mole, a type of sauce used in Mexican cuisine, gets its name from the Nahuatl word *molli*.

The Toltecs decorated their temples with beautiful statues and carvings.

The Toltecs had been the last of the powerful Mesoamericans, before the rise of the Aztecs. Around 1150, Toltec noble families moved farther south into the Valley of Mexico. The wandering tribes that settled in the valley saw the powerful state the Toltecs had once ruled. New leaders from the migrating tribes tried to marry into Toltec families, so they could claim a tie to the Toltec civilization. One of the ruling families with such a tie to the Toltecs controlled the town of Culhuacan. That place would play an important role in Mexica history.

Once in the Valley of Mexico, the Mexica struggled to acquire land because the earlier migrants were more powerful and drove them away. The people of Culhuacan defeated the Mexica at one battle, forcing the group to move again. Some Mexica leaders begged the rulers of Culhuacan to have pity on them. The rulers agreed to let the Mexica settle on marshy land at a place called Tizaapan. The waters were filled with snakes and were not a welcoming spot for the Mexica. Grateful for the land, however, they settled in Tizaapan and tried to build a new home.

To get food, the Mexica learned to hunt the snakes and other reptiles living in the marshes. The settlers also farmed. The Mexica developed close ties to the people of Culhuacan, helping them fight their enemies. This connection with Culhuacan made the Mexica believe their ties to the Toltecs were growing. They tried to make it stronger by having a princess from Culhuacan become their queen and the wife of their god Huitzilopochtli. Becoming his wife, however, meant that she had to be **sacrificed** to the gods. When

sacrificed (SAK-ruh-fised) killed as an offering to a god

This nineteenth-century painting depicts the Mexica arriving at Lake Texcoco after leaving Tizaapan.

15

the Culhuacans learned of the princess's death, they attacked the Mexica and drove them from Tizaapan. Wanderers again, in 1325 the Mexica settled on an island in Lake Texcoco.

THE FOUNDING OF TENOCHTITLAN

Once more, Huitzilopochtli would lead the Mexica to a new home. The priests said that on the island, the Mexica would see an eagle sitting on a nopal, or prickly pear cactus, that grew out of a rock. Sure enough, the Mexica saw the eagle on the cactus, and they built a temple to honor Huitzilopochtli. That spot became the center of their new home, the city of Tenochtitlan. In the Aztec language of Nahuatl, the name means "among the stone-cactus fruit."

The location was not perfect. The Mexica struggled at first to grow crops and find supplies to build homes. But they were able to catch fish and hunt birds and animals that lived along the water. This provided enough food for themselves and enough to sell at markets in nearby towns. The Mexica built a second city on the island, which they called Tlatelolco. It became the site of another market, which developed into the largest in the Valley of Mexico. The people of the two cities also built special gardens called chinampas, which produced corn, squash, and other crops.

The Tepanecs, one of the earlier migrating tribes from the north, controlled the area around the Mexica's new home. The Tepanecs required the Mexica to supply warriors for their battles against other tribes. Under Tezozomoc, their ruler, the Tepanecs extended their control across large parts of the Valley of Mexico. To reward the Mexica for their military service, Tezozomoc let them fight on their own and collect tribute from the towns they defeated. This new wealth helped strengthen the Mexica.

Aztec legends claim that the Mexica chose the site for Tenochtitlan after seeing an eagle perched upon a cactus.

This statue was discovered at the site of the ancient city of Texcoco.

NEW KING, NEW ALLIES

In about 1375, the Mexica acquired their own *tlatoani*, or leader. The honor went to Acamapichtli, the son of a leading Mexica and a Culhuacan princess. Despite the past conflicts with the Culhuacans, the two groups had once again forged friendly relations. Over the next few decades, the Mexica strengthened their ties to the royalty of Culhuacan and Azcapotzalco, the capital of the Tepanecs. For example, Chimalpopoca, the third Mexica king, was the grandson of Tezozomoc. Through royal marriage, the Mexica were also allied with Texcoco, a city to the east of the lake with the same name. Like the Mexica, the people of Texcoco were part of the small but growing state under Tepanec control.

The Tepanecs were thrown into confusion with the death of Tezozomoc in 1426. Two of his sons struggled to control the throne. Meanwhile, the new Mexica tlatoani, Itzcoatl, organized a rebellion against the Tepanecs. He convinced the cities of Texcoco and Tlacopan to become allies in a battle against the new Tepanec king. They defeated the Tepanecs, and in 1428 the three cities created the Triple Alliance. This was another name for the Aztec Empire that was soon to emerge. The leaders of the three cities agreed that Tenochtitlan and Texcoco would each get 40 percent of whatever tributes the alliance won through conquest. The Tlacopan would get the rest.

The Triple Alliance decided that the new empire would do whatever was necessary to survive and grow. There would be battles, of course, but the Aztecs would seek to build ties through royal marriage, as the Mexica had done. The Aztecs would also link the distant people they conquered through trade. The rulers would build temples and pyramids in the places where they held religious festivals. These actions would please the gods and connect the Aztec rulers to those gods in the eyes of their **subjects**.

Some honored Aztec warriors belonged to the Order of the Jaguar Knights.

A Growing Empire

On the battlefield, the Aztecs first made sure they kept control over the cities the Tepanecs ruled. Especially important were towns to the south, which had many chinampas that provided food. In 1440, Montezuma I became the tlatoani of Tenochtitlan. Under his rule, the Triple Alliance spread its control outside the Valley of Mexico. Aztec forces conquered lands to the east, all the way to the Gulf of Mexico. In one battle against the Huaxtecs, the Aztecs surprised their enemy warriors and either killed them or took them prisoner. Then the Aztecs entered their enemy's city and burned the temple, killing old and young alike. After their battles, the

porters (POR-turz)
people who carry
equipment on an
expedition or military
mission

Aztecs marched their prisoners back to Tenochtitlan, where they were sacrificed to the gods.

In another successful military venture, Montezuma organized an army of twenty thousand men to fight the Mixtecs to the south. Ten thousand **porters** marched with the Aztec warriors. The Aztecs had no pack animals, such as horses or cattle, to carry the food and weapons the soldiers needed. They also did not have wagons. The porters hauled the supplies on their backs, using a wooden frame called a *cacaxtli* to hold the items.

Defeated enemies, such as the Mixtecs, agreed to give tribute to the Aztecs several times during the year. The Aztecs sought luxury goods, such as fine blankets. They also desired food that they could not grow close to Tenochtitlan, such as cacao beans, the source of chocolate. After their defeat, the Mixtecs' tribute included bowls of gold dust.

During the first decades of the Triple Alliance, the city of Tlatelolco remained independent from Tenochtitlan, with its own tlatoani. But in 1473, the two cities that shared an island and cultural roots fought each other. A dispute between their related royal families played a part. Tenochtitlan won the battle, and from then on, its tlatoani controlled the entire island.

The Aztecs were not always victorious in battle. Around 1478, the tlatoani Axayacatl launched a war against the Tarascans, who lived just to the west of Aztec-controlled lands. Having built their own powerful state, the Tarascans were a threat to Aztec interests in the region. Some historical sources say that the Aztecs amassed a fighting force of twenty-four thousand warriors to challenge the Tarascans. Their enemy, however, had an even larger army and defeated the Aztecs. Relations remained tense between these two peoples.

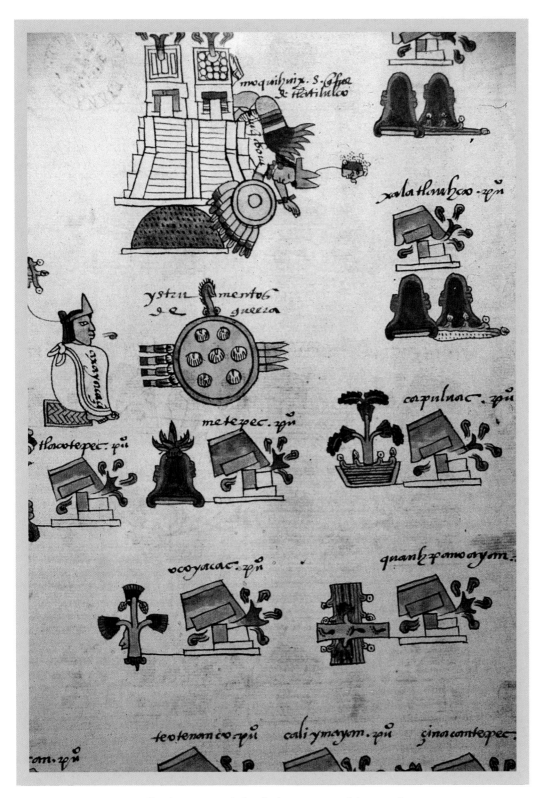

This Aztec artwork details the conquests of Axayacatl.

This sixteenth-century painting shows what Montezuma II might have looked like.

THE AZTECS AT THEIR HEIGHT

Despite their loss to the Tarascans, the Aztecs continued to expand their influence. Under the tlatoani Ahuitzotl, who began his rule in 1486, they gained control of the Valley of Oaxaca, south of the Valley of Mexico. They also received tribute from peoples who lived along the Pacific Ocean. Ahuitzotl conquered towns along the frontier that lay next to Tarascan land, in order to strengthen the border with his enemy. To ensure the loyalty of these new towns, Ahuitzotl killed all the adults and sent the children to live in Aztec cities. Then thousands of Aztecs from Tenochtitlan and other cities moved into the border towns.

During Ahuitzotl's rule, the tlatoani of Tenochtitlan became the supreme leader of the Triple Alliance. The once-wandering Mexica were now in charge of the greatest empire in central Mexico. In 1502, Montezuma II, great-grandson of the first Montezuma, took control of the empire. His wars strengthened control over any areas that tried to rebel and added new lands to the south.

Montezuma II also fought the Tlaxcalans. These Nahuatl-speaking people to the east of Tenochtitlan had never come under Aztec rule, even as the Aztecs surrounded the lands the Tlaxcalans controlled. Constant fighting with Tlaxcala provided the Aztecs with a steady source of sacrifice victims—and stirred deep hatred of the Aztecs in Tlaxcala. Despite his army's strength, however, Montezuma II could not hold off the Tlaxcalans. When the Spaniards arrived in 1519, the Tlaxcalans became their allies against Montezuma II. Together, Europeans and Mexicans would end Aztec power in the Valley of Mexico.

CHAPTER TWO

RULING THE AZTEC EMPIRE

Montezuma II stood on the pyramid as the people of
Tenochtitlan watched silently from below. Trumpets blared
as the Aztec noble prepared to begin his coronation, the

Aztec nobles surround Montezuma II as he was confirmed as tlatoani of Tenochtitlan.

ceremony that officially made him tlatoani of the empire. The coronation lasted for several days, and in the end, the Aztecs saw Montezuma as something greater than a mere human. He was connected to the gods and almost a god himself.

THE TLATOANI

Before there was an Aztec Empire, the Mexica and other migrants from the north had strong ideas about who should rule them. The gods, they believed, had made some people superior to others. These were the nobles of Mexica society. They were thought to be related to one of two major gods, Quetzalcoatl or Xiuhtecuhtli, the Mexica fire god. All Mexica rulers had to come from noble families.

The cities of the Triple Alliance, and smaller cities within the empire, were known as *altepetl*. They were what today are sometimes called city-states: a powerful core city with surrounding villages that were associated with it. Each altepetl had its own supreme tlatoani. For part of Aztec history, the tlatoani of Tenochtitlan ruled as the emperor of the Aztec lands.

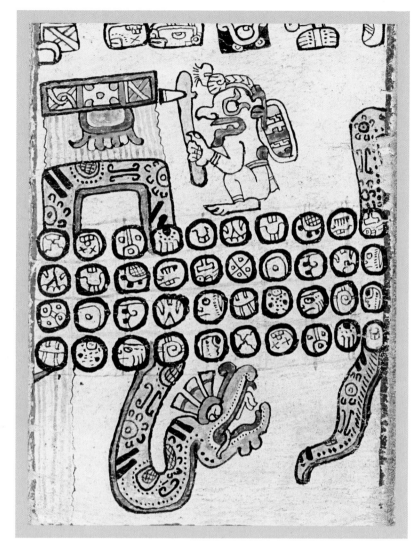

Quetzalcoatl was represented as a feathered serpent.

Mexica history says that a chieftain named Tenoch served as leader of the tribe when it reached Tenochtitlan in 1325. Tenoch was supposedly elected by a group of nobles, whom he consulted before making decisions. Some modern historians, however, consider Tenoch a legendary figure. They claim Acamapichtli was the first true tlatoani. The tlatoque (plural of "tlatoani") in most cities consulted with nobles and at times with warriors and priests. When one altepetl defeated another, the winning side let the losing tlatoani stay in power—as long as the loser agreed to accept the authority of the winning side. The defeated ruler also had to make sure his people paid the tribute they owed the victors.

The Past Is Present
SEEING RED

Spanish conquest of the Aztec Empire in the sixteenth century introduced Europeans to an extraordinary deep red dye. The only red dye the Europeans knew was a paler color made from a plant extract called madder red. The secret to the Aztecs' rich red dye was a tiny beetle called the cochineal. The beetle's body consists largely of an acid that produces the red dye. About seventy thousand bugs were

needed for every pound of dye that was made. The Spaniards began exporting the dye back home, where it became an important part of their economy. Because it was so expensive to produce, the dye was used only for royalty, religious figures, and military officers. Today, chemical dyes have largely replaced the cochineal as a fabric dye, but the insect is still used throughout the world to make a dye in cosmetics and as a food coloring. Mexico, Chile, and Peru are major exporters of the dye to countries such as France, Japan, and Italy.

The word *tlatoani* means "speaker." In a sense, the tlatoani spoke for all his people in dealing with other tribes. The Aztec emperor was called the *huey*, or great, speaker. In essence, the first tlatoque were the commanders in chief of the Mexica during wartime. Over time, they took on other duties, including religious ones. The tlatoani performed a **rite** designed to ask the gods for rain and made decisions for the community based on signs in nature thought to reflect the gods' desires.

BECOMING A TLATOANI

Male members of the royal family elected the Aztec tlatoani. The new ruler was usually a son or brother of the previous one. Once elected, the new tlatoani was officially given the power to rule. The coronation ceremony was a key event in the life of a tlatoani.

rite (RITE) a religious event or activity with special meaning

By becoming king of his people, the ruler was taking on a serious responsibility. He would face troubles in Tenochtitlan and have to fight foreign wars. His people expected him to rule wisely, seek the truth, and, according to one record of a coronation speech, "put forth all thy effort, give all, put forth all thy spirit."

At the coronation ceremony, the new tlatoani first took off all his noble clothing and wore a simple **loincloth**. With this act, the emperor-to-be cast aside his past as a wealthy and powerful member of society. As part of the ceremony, the tlatoani cut himself to offer his blood to the gods.

loincloth (LOYN-klawth) garment worn around a man's waist

The coronation marked the official beginning of a tlatoani's rule.

On the fifth day after the coronation, the tlatoque of neighboring Texcoco and Tlacopan put a gold crown on the new emperor and adorned him with gold jewelry. After many speeches, the new tlatoani gave gifts to nobles and warriors. The guests then had a huge feast. But the coronation was still not over. Although chosen by the gods to rule, the new tlatoani still had to prove his skills on the battlefield. War was a crucial part of Aztec life, since it brought wealth to the empire and provided the victims needed for sacrifices.

For his coronation war, Montezuma II led an army about 400 miles (644 kilometers) to the south of Tenochtitlan. The towns in the region, called Nopallan and Icpatepec, had built strong forts to resist such an attack. The Aztecs, however, used ladders to climb up the enemies' walls. Montezuma II won his war and demanded tribute. He also took prisoners back to Tenochtitlan.

Some coronation wars, however, were not as successful. Tizoc, who ruled for only five years (1481–1486), almost lost his first war. The enemy was ready for the advancing Aztec army and dealt them heavy losses. Tizoc returned home with only forty prisoners, and his struggle was seen as a bad **omen**. A weak ruler and commander, Tizoc was possibly poisoned by nobles who opposed him.

THE CIHUACOATL

The tlatoani of the Aztecs shared ruling powers with a *cihuacoatl*. The Mexica had a goddess of the same name, which meant "woman serpent." The cihuacoatl, however, was always a man. This position seemed to have the most power in Tenochtitlan, compared to other city-states in the Valley of Mexico.

The cihuacoatl was in charge of the affairs within the city-state and may have rarely left the main urban area. His duties included

This carving of the Aztec rulers Tizoc and Ahuitzotl dates to 1487 CE.

running the altepetl when the commander was away at war and serving as a judge in major court cases. The cihuacoatl also gave advice on military strategy and received a share of the tribute that came from defeated peoples. The cihuacoatl played a role in some religious rites as well. It was his duty to arrange the sacrifice of foreign prisoners.

Under Montezuma II, the office of cihuacoatl lost some power, as the tlatoani wanted to control more of the government himself. The Spaniards, however, kept the position for a short time after they ended Montezuma's rule. The last cihuacoatl, Tlacotzin, was chosen in 1524.

GOVERNING A NATION

No one person or even a handful of nobles could rule an empire as vast as that of the Aztecs. The tlatoque relied on a number of people to keep the peace and keep tribute flowing to their palaces. Aztec rulers usually let local kings remain in control of their lands, as long as they were loyal to Tenochtitlan. In some cases, however, the Aztecs might replace an unfriendly king with someone from the same royal family who would obey their orders. In rare cases, the Aztecs put their own ruler in charge of a defeated altepetl.

provinces (PRAH-vihn-sez) districts or regions of some countries

The **provinces** closest to Tenochtitlan provided tribute of all kinds. Strategic provinces sat along the border with the empire's enemies. They provided military defense against possible attack, and some also sent prisoners to Tenochtitlan for sacrifices. In some outer provinces, the Aztecs kept their own troops to prevent enemy attacks. The Aztec military presence would also ensure that the local people did not rebel.

Throughout the empire, tax collectors called the *calpixque* were important government officials. They made sure the various towns paid their tribute. The tribute collected by the calpixque went to the emperor, but local residents often had to pay other kinds of tribute. Some went to the tlatoani of their city-states, and the rest was given to local nobles. Some people, however, did not have to pay tribute. These included nobles, priests, merchants, and teachers.

Within towns and villages, a *calpulli* was the smallest political unit. The first *calpultin* (plural of "calpulli") were clans, or groups of related people. Over time, a calpulli became a neighborhood that contained residents who were not necessarily related to each other. Its leader was elected by the elder men of the calpulli. A new leader was often the son or another relative of the man who held the position before him. This leader made sure that the calpulli paid the tribute it owed and organized residents to carry out building projects. Each calpulli also educated the local children.

From the small scale of the local calpultin to the far-reaching rule of an empire, the Aztecs built and maintained a system of government that resulted in an orderly life for the average citizen.

CHAPTER THREE

LAKES, MOUNTAINS, AND RESOURCES

A ccording to their legends, the Mexica came from an island in the middle of a lake. After their years of wandering, they made their new home on another island. This island sat high above sea level—even the lowest points in the Valley of Mexico are more than 7,000 feet (2,134 meters) high.

THE VALLEY OF MEXICO

People first settled in the Valley of Mexico thousands of years before the Aztecs arrived. The valley is surrounded by three different mountain ranges. To the west of Tenochtitlan (present-day Mexico City) is the **Sierra** de las Cruces and to the east is the Sierra Nevada. The Sierra Nevada contain the two tallest mountains in the region, Popo and Ixta. These nicknames come from their original Nahuatl names, Popocatépetl and Iztaccíhuatl. Popo, an active volcano, measures 17,802 feet (5,426 m) tall. Ixta, a

dormant volcano, reaches up 17,126 feet (5,220 m). More volcanoes can be found in the Sierra Ajusco, a southern mountain range in the Valley of Mexico.

Above roughly 13,000 feet (3,962 m), the climate on the mountains was too harsh for the early settlers to live. But trees grew in the higher elevations, and the Aztecs used them for lumber and charcoal. The trees included pine, fir, and oak. The volcanoes of the region also played a part in providing resources. Ancient eruptions deposited minerals on the soil that made it ideal for growing crops. Snows that fell in the mountains provided water for crops and the people in the valley below.

Popo (pictured) is still an active volcano, while Ixta lies dormant.

sierra (see-ER-uh) a chain of hills or mountains with peaks that look like sharp, jagged teeth

dormant (DOR-muhnt) a volcano that is not doing anything now but could erupt again

ISLANDS OF PLENTY

For a people who had little farmable land, but were surrounded by water, the Aztecs' chinampas were the perfect solution for growing crops. The Spaniards called the chinampas "floating gardens," but they really didn't float. The Mexica gathered soil from beneath the marshes, along with water plants, to build long, earthen islands in the water. On the sides of the islands,

the Mexica installed wooden posts with vines and branches tied to them. This helped keep the soil in place, as did willow trees planted next to the islands. The tops of the islands rose above the

water's surface so seeds could be planted in them. Canals ran between the chinampas in which canoes could move to take the harvest from the islands. Chinampas provided up to half of the crops eaten each year in Tenochtitlan, and they are still used to grow crops in Mexico's Lake Xochimilco.

The valley itself contained several different landforms. In some places, particularly to the north, the land was flat. Other regions were hilly, especially near the foot of the mountains. Outside the Valley of Mexico were several other valleys.

A CHALLENGING CLIMATE

The mountains ringing the Valley of Mexico play a part in the region's climate. Starting in late May or June, warm, wet air begins to blow in from the Gulf of Mexico. The warm air rises to the mountain peaks, and then begins to cool in the colder temperatures of the higher elevations. This leads to the creation of storm clouds, which bring heavy rains to the valley. In a typical year, the valley receives between 23 and 27 inches (58 and 69 centimeters) of rain. Most of it falls during the summer rainy season.

The climate was a constant concern for some Aztec farmers. Frost could damage crops at the beginning and the end of the growing season, especially at higher elevations. If the summer rains didn't come, the **drought** that followed could wipe out the crops, as happened during the **famines** of the 1450s. Families were forced to sell themselves into slavery in places unaffected by the famine. The northern part of the valley was drier than the rest. It was more difficult to grow crops there, even when the rains arrived elsewhere in the valley. Drought was less common in the empire's lands outside of the valley, especially in **tropical** climates and at lower elevations.

PRODUCTS FROM THE EARTH

Even with an uncertain climate, the Aztecs were able to feed a growing empire. At times, they built dams to collect water and then dug canals to direct the water to their fields. Some people

drought (DROUT) a long period without rain

famines (FAM-inz) serious lack of food in a geographic area

tropical (TRAH-pi-kuhl) of or having to do with the hot, rainy areas close to the equator

The Aztecs relied on good weather for their crops to grow.

built terraces on hills to increase the land they could farm. The terrace was a flat area of land edged with a stone wall.

Corn, or maize, was the most important food grown in the empire. It grew at almost any elevation, and in some regions outside the Valley of Mexico, farmers could plant and harvest corn twice a year. Corn was one of many crops that were **domesticated** in Mesoamerica before the rise of the Aztecs. In fact, farmers

were growing corn in Mexico by about six thousand years ago. Many of the other foods domesticated in the region are still enjoyed around the world today, such as squash, beans, chili peppers, and a grain called amaranth.

One important crop for the Aztecs was the agave, sometimes called the century plant. Agave can grow at high altitudes and in poor soil. The plant also does well without water and can stand cold temperatures. The agave provided a sap that the Aztecs made into a drink called *pulque*. They also ate its roots and large leaves. The plant provided a white fiber that the Aztecs used in many ways. The fiber, called *ixtle*, was used to

This twentieth-century painting by Diego Rivera depicts the Aztecs creating a variety of products from agave.

make clothing, rope, fishing nets, sandals, sewing thread, and other items. The leaves and stalks of the agave were used as building material. Native peoples even used the plant's thorns as pins. Ixtle is used in parts of Mexico today, to make cloths used to carry items on a person's back. Alcoholic beverages are made from agave, and the sap the plant produces is used as a sweetener.

The prickly pear cactus was another plant raised as food. But cacti had other uses in Aztec society. Tall, thin cacti were sometimes

Archaeologists have discovered the hardened remains of tzictli from hundreds of years ago.

planted in a row to make a fence around a farm or to mark a boundary. The plants are still used that way today in parts of central Mexico. In the Aztec system of writing, which used pictures called glyphs, a cactus represented the city of Tenochtitlan. The image referred to the legendary founding of the city on a spot where the Mexica saw an eagle sitting on a nopal that grew from a rock.

Like other Mexicans before them, the Aztecs chewed gum, which they called *tzictli*. It came from the *chicozapote* tree, which provided a fruit, leaves for tea, and was the source of building materials. Tzictli may have been the source of the Spanish word for "gum," *chicle*, which is the root of the Chiclets brand of gum sold today. The sixteenth-century Spaniard Bernardino de Sahagún wrote that Aztec women chewed chicle to get rid of the bad odor of their mouths or the bad smell of their teeth.

Although the Aztecs relied heavily on crops for food, they ate three domesticated animals: turkeys, dogs, and ducks. The people of the Valley of Mexico also hunted a variety of wild animals. They used the animals for meat and made their skins and fur into clothing. Rabbit fur was used to make capes, and both deer and jaguar skins were used to make clothing. Aztecs ate rabbit, deer, and several types of birds. Other wildlife in Aztec lands included monkeys, parrots and other tropical birds, and eagles. The Aztecs associated the eagle with the sun and with great fighting skills.

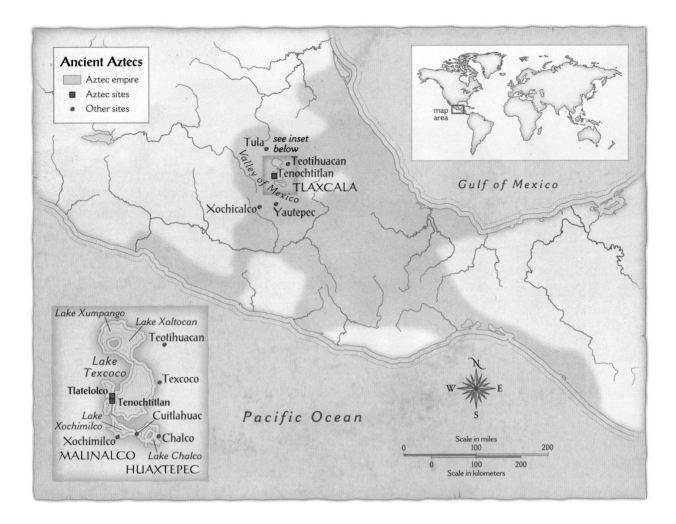

THE LAKES OF THE VALLEY

Surrounded by water in Tenochtitlan, the Mexica and the other
tribes around them used the lakes of the Valley of Mexico as a
source of food. In their canoes, Aztecs transported goods and mes-
sages across long distances.

The five main lakes around Tenochtitlan were, from north to
south, Xumpango, Xaltocan, Texcoco, Xochimilco, and Chalco.
The lakes were connected, but their waters were different. The
two northern lakes were freshwater, while Lake Texcoco was salty.
Xochimilco and Chalco were fed by freshwater springs. The waters

The Aztecs dug canals to create waterways, as shown in this nineteenth-century illustration.

of Xochimilco and Chalco were suitable for growing crops, so these lakes were the site of large, productive chinampas. The lakes could also flood after heavy rains. To protect Tenochtitlan from flooding, the Aztecs built a **dike** about 9 miles (14.5 km) long. They also built canals so boats could move freely through the city. Three causeways, or roads built on beds of stone or earth, linked Tenochtitlan to the mainland beyond the lakes. Although suitable for growing crops, Lake Texcoco was too salty to use as a source of drinking water. The Aztecs built stone structures called aqueducts that carried water from distant springs into Tenochtitlan.

PRODUCTS FROM THE LAKES

The major lakes in the Valley of Mexico served as a source of food and other resources, as did the coastal waters at the edges of the empire. The Aztecs fished and hunted frogs and turtles, as well as shellfish such as oysters and clams. They mixed a dough with an aquatic insect called an *axayacatl* to make a food of the same name. Fishermen used nets to catch the bugs, which were then dried in the sun. The dried insects were mashed and mixed with water and wrapped in husks of corn, similar to the way tamales are made today. The eggs of the axayacatl were a special treat. After being collected from the leaves of plants, they were pressed into a brick and dried. The food would last for months without spoiling. Today, these eggs are used in some pet foods.

The waters of the valley produced other goods as well. Reeds that grew by the water were used to make a mat called *petlatl*. Modern-day Mexicans still use these mats and call them petates. Soil found near Lake Texcoco was mixed with water and left to dry. The salt in the soil was then removed and used in food preparation.

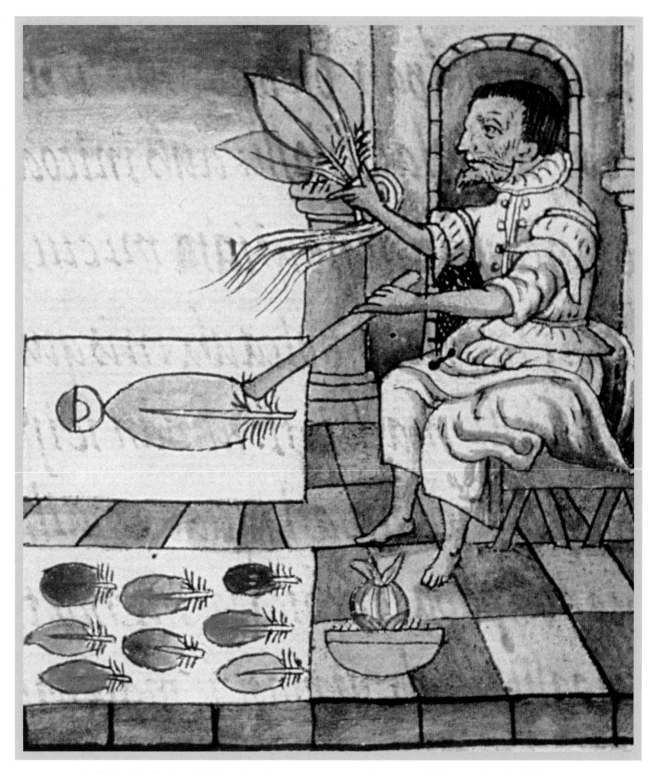

As depicted in this Spanish illustration, Aztec artisans created a variety of objects using colorful feathers.

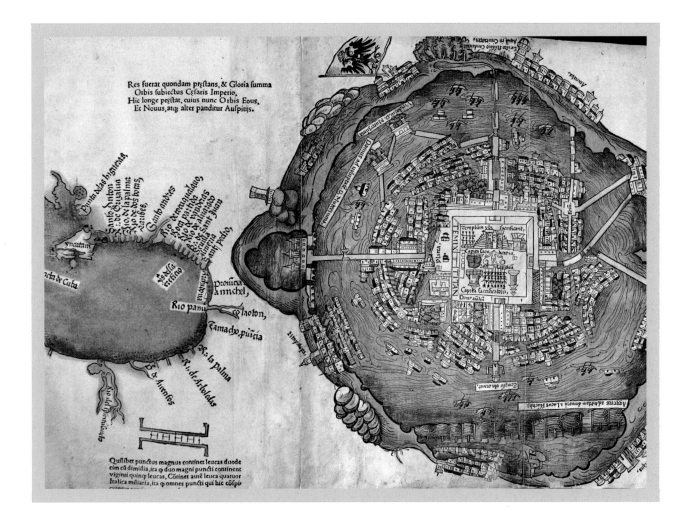

This sixteenth-century map shows the waters surrounding Tenochtitlan.

The shells from shellfish were sometimes made into jewelry. Large conch shells had a small opening on one end and a larger opening on the other. Blowing into the small hole produced a loud noise, so the shells were used as horns in religious rites or during battle.

From the Valley of Mexico to the edges of their empire, the Aztecs found lands rich in natural resources. Their farming techniques made the land even more productive, although those skills could not prevent droughts and other natural disasters that affected crops.

45

CHAPTER FOUR

LIVING IN THE AZTEC EMPIRE

In the bustling market of Tlatelolco, merchants sold a variety of goods. In the temples of Tenochtitlan, priests prepared for religious rites. In towns and villages across the empire, men worked in the

This exhibit at the Field Museum in Chicago, Illinois, imagines what the market of Tlatelolco may have looked like.

This page from the Florentine Codex, a sixteenth-century study of the Aztecs by the Spanish, depicts Aztec nobles with their children.

fields while women sat at looms, weaving cloth for their families and to sell at the market. During wartime, the men left their fields to fight for the local nobles, who in turn served the emperor.

The Aztecs had a very clear social order, with a small group of nobles and royalty having the highest status. Known as the *pipil-tin*, they controlled most of the wealth and power in society. They

Rulers and their families occupied the highest positions in Aztec society.

passed their wealth and their high social rank on to their children. The pipiltin also included many Aztec priests. Most people were commoners, or *macehualtin*. In between the two groups, were the *pochteca*, or merchants. Although merchants were commoners, they could amass great riches as they carried out trade across the empire. At the bottom of society were *tlatlacotin*, or slaves.

LIFE AT THE TOP

The social classes of the Aztec civilization have been compared to a pointed pyramid, with a wide base of commoners supporting the much smaller group of nobles and royalty above it. At the very top, of course, was the tlatoani of Tenochtitlan. Immediately below him were the kings of the other city-states, and then nobles called *tecuhtli*, who held top military and political positions. They controlled large areas of land. The families of the kings and highest nobles made up the rest of the pipiltin.

As a group, the pipiltin had the largest homes, ate the best food, and wore the finest clothes. Laws created under Montezuma I described what kinds of homes each class could own and what those people could wear. Montezuma said noblemen and warriors were allowed to build homes with two stories. Anyone disobeying this rule could be put to death. A noble's house might feature carefully cut stones and walls made with plaster, a mixture of water, sand, and minerals.

The Past Is Present
REVIVING THE PAST

Aztec architecture possessed a strong sense of symbolism, order, and balance. The geometric patterns and designs, as well as the long sweeping lines used in their architecture, were representations of the Aztecs' religious and cultural beliefs. The Aztecs communicated these beliefs on walls, in plazas, and with ornate stone carvings. Their architectural stylings were used in pyramids, temples, marketplaces, gardens, and ball courts, where athletes competed.

The Aztec Revival architectural movement of the 1920s and 1930s drew heavily from Mexica and Aztec influences. Thousands of Aztec Revival buildings still stand today. The Guardian Building (left) in Detroit, Michigan, and the Imperial Hotel in Tokyo, Japan, are outstanding examples of this style.

This page from the Florentine Codex *depicts Aztec nobles living in elaborate homes and eating quality foods.*

Montezuma's laws stated that only the nobles could wear cotton. Commoners had to wear clothing made from ixtle or other fibers. Within the noble class, only the highest-ranking members could wear certain colors and designs. Nobles were the only ones who could wear jewelry made from gold and the finest gems.

When the Spaniards arrived, they often noted how clean Montezuma II was—he took a bath at least once a day. For many Europeans of the time, such cleanliness was uncommon. The habits of good **hygiene** didn't stop with the nobles. Most Aztecs were careful to wash their hair, bathe, and clean their teeth on a regular basis. They used various plants to clean themselves. Charcoal was used as a type of toothbrush. The Aztecs also built bathhouses, where hot water created steam that could be used to both clean and soothe a tired body.

hygiene (HYE-jeen) keeping yourself and the things around you clean, in order to stay healthy

MANY KINDS OF COMMONERS

Historians think that as many as 90 percent of the Aztec population was macehualtin. Within that group were several distinct classes. At the bottom were slaves. A person usually became a slave to pay off a debt owed to someone else, as punishment for a crime, or after being taken prisoner in battle. Slaves could own property and marry a free person, and the children of slaves were free.

Next were the *mayeque*, the peasants who worked the land for great nobles. They were forbidden to leave the land to work for someone else or to buy their own land. Their children were also tied to the land in this way. Mayeque could be required to serve in the military, as were macehualtin.

The great mass of macehualtin worked on land owned by the nobles, in the palaces, or in the markets. These commoners had to pay the tribute that went to local nobles and to the emperor. Some of them built the grand palaces and temples of the major cities.

Each free *macehualli* (singular of "macehualtin") belonged to a calpulli, and the leaders of each calpulli decided who would farm which plot of land. A farmer and his family did not own the land themselves. It belonged to the local nobles or to the city-state.

Not all people farmed, however. The Aztecs relied on a number of skilled workers and **artisans** to design their buildings and create luxury items for the nobles. These people included stoneworkers, carpenters, potters, and basket makers. The most respected artisans crafted the things the Aztecs valued most, such as jewelry made of gold and gems and feathered items. Groups of goldsmiths or feather workers often lived together in their own neighborhoods and formed their own calpulli. A skilled artisan could become very wealthy.

LONG-DISTANCE TRADERS

Anyone could sell goods they made or crops they raised at a local market. Some markets became known for selling a particular item, such as wood products or cloth. Other merchants bought goods from the people who made them and then traveled to different markets in a region. A pochteca was a special kind of trader, one who traveled long distances across the empire and beyond, to search for exotic goods. Although they were not pipiltin, these merchants received special rights from the emperor. The pochteca did not have to perform work for the tlatoani, though they did pay a tax on their goods. Pochteca could pass on their jobs to their sons. The emperor chose the traders who supervised the other pochteca. These traders received special clothing to mark their

Aztecs of all classes practiced good hygiene.

distinction from other commoners. The emperors relied on them to not only bring luxury goods to Tenochtitlan, but sometimes to spy on foreign lands and serve as warriors.

The role of the pochteca also had religious importance. Certain pochteca were slave traders, and they took part in a ceremony honoring the god Huitzilopochtli. Slave traders washed the slaves used in sacrifices. Younger traders were responsible for obtaining gifts given to special guests at the ceremony.

obsidian (uhb-SID-
ee-uhn) a shiny, usually
black glass created by
volcanic activity

Special rites marked the beginning of the pochteca's trade journeys. The merchants washed their hair and cut it for the last time until they returned home. On a wooden stick they carried, the merchants wrapped images of certain gods, which would protect the pochteca during their travels. The merchants also cut themselves, so they could offer some of their blood to the gods.

WARRIORS

In their quest for more tribute, the tlatoani of the Aztecs relied on the skills of their warriors. Warriors came from both the commoner and noble classes, though the top generals were nobles. For commoners, success in battle was the major way to win respect in Aztec society. For each enemy soldier taken alive in battle, the Aztec soldier received an honor, such as a special weapon or clothing decorated with feathers. If a soldier captured four enemies, he could wear the skin of a jaguar. The large cat was called an *ocelotl*, a Nahuatl word that is the source of the English word *ocelot*. Other soldiers who performed well in battle wore eagle feathers and helmets shaped like an eagle's head. The eagle and jaguar societies were formed of the best soldiers in the Aztec army. They received special privileges, which included wearing cotton clothing.

In a typical battle, each side first launched arrows and fired rocks with slingshots. The Aztecs also used a spear thrower called an *atlatl* that added extra force when throwing a large dart or small spear. After an exchange of missiles, the two sides fought hand to hand. Weapons included clubs and swords with **obsidian** blades. At times, the Aztecs dug holes and hid in them, and then jumped out and surprised the approaching enemy. The Aztecs shouted wildly as they fought, trying to stir fear among their enemy.

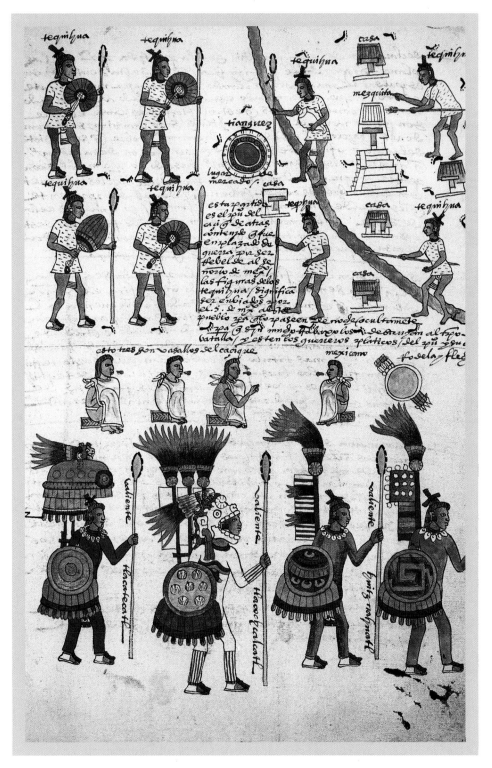

Aztec warriors often carried shields into battle.

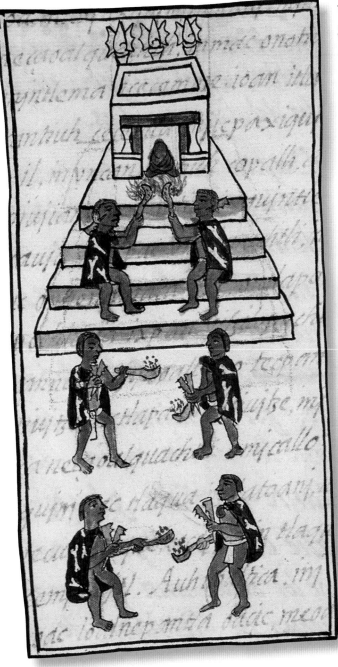

Aztec priests performed a variety of religious ceremonies.

The Aztecs won many battles because they outnumbered their foes, but they were also famous for their bravery. One Spaniard wrote that he was impressed with how the Aztecs "face death with absolute determination," with one Aztec battling several Spaniards at once.

PRIESTS

Like warriors, priests were an important part of Aztec life. The highest priests were nobility, but some commoners also joined this privileged class. The two highest priests were associated with the Aztecs' two most important gods, Huitzilopochtli and Tlaloc, the god of rain. The priests took care of the temples of these gods at Tenochtitlan. Other priests watched over the temples and ran the schools that educated young priests. Some priests had special skills. Some were scribes and others were astronomers who tracked the movement of the stars and planets. Some priests also served as warriors. Certain high priests played a major role in sacrifices during religious ceremonies. Women served as priestesses and worked in temples, and took part in different feasts and ceremonies.

DAILY LIFE

There were great extremes of wealth and power in Aztec society. Some parts of daily life, however, were the same for most people throughout the empire. For example, almost everyone slept on petlatls, or reed mats. The wealthy might use a pile of them, rather than using the single mat a commoner would. Everyone kept their personal belongings in boxes. A commoner's box or chest was made of reeds, while nobles used wooden chests. Montezuma II had large chests to hold his valued possessions.

Scribes and artists helped keep records of Aztec history.

Aztec women used looms to weave cloth.

In the commoners' homes, men and women had specific jobs, but they were considered equal partners in most things. Men worked the fields, fished, or practiced a craft, while women took care of the home. Men were the warriors, but women were known to defend their towns with weapons if they came under attack. Women could own property and work outside the home, selling goods in the market or serving as healers. They also collected the sap from agave plants to use to make pulque, a beverage still drunk today in parts of Mexico. Women played a role in medicine as well. Trained women called midwives helped other women have babies, and some women healed the sick with plants and herbs, as did trained men. Modern science has shown that many of the natural treatments the Aztecs used contain chemicals that work the way modern medicines do.

The most common food the Aztecs ate was corn. Women spent many hours preparing it to be used to make tortillas and tamales, foods still enjoyed to this day. The cooks kneeled behind a stone grinding surface called a *metate* and used a grinding stone called a *mano* to roll out *masa harina*, or corn dough. Sauces with beans, tomatoes, chilies, and various kinds of meat added extra flavor to the corn dishes.

Another important job for women was weaving cloth. Even the wealthiest noblewomen learned this skill. The cloth they made on their looms was used to make capes and loincloths for men and skirts and blouses for women. Using dyed thread or paint, weavers created different patterns in the cloth. When collecting tribute, the Aztecs often demanded cloth, and cloth was also used as a form of money in the markets.

The typical woman's daily activities took place in a small home made of adobe bricks, which were molded from clay and straw. The walls were built on a foundation of stones. A peasant's home often had two doors but no windows. Sometimes two to five homes were built close together and shared a common open area between the buildings. In towns and cities, commoners built their homes around a central area that housed the most important buildings. These included a temple and the palace of the local tla-toani. The central area also included an open space called a plaza.

A Child's Life

An Aztec girl was trained at an early age for the chores that awaited her when she was older. Boys, too, learned their specific roles when they were young. At birth, children received gifts that reflected what they would do when they grew up. A baby girl received a broom, fiber that would be spun into thread, and tools used to spin the thread. Baby boys received tools like the ones their father used at work: carpenter's tools, for example, or the weapons of a warrior.

At three years old, Aztec children began helping around the house. By seven, a boy would go out with his father to learn how to fish, while a girl learned how to spin thread and cook. The children did more work on their own as they grew older. Noble parents stressed how their children should behave outside the house. The children were to speak slowly and clearly. The nobles also taught their children to dress well, obey orders, and not spread rumors. Children of all classes were taught the value of hard work and of not bragging. Those who disobeyed might be pricked with cactus needles as punishment. Older boys who misbehaved were forced to inhale the smoke of burning chilies.

A child's life was not only about discipline and work. At an early age, children were taught dances and singing, and participated in community gatherings. Children also played a game similar to today's pillow fights, with boys filling sacks with soft items and then using them to playfully hit girls. The girls fought back by chasing the boys with cactus thorns. Other Aztec games included one with marbles and another that is like the modern game of jacks.

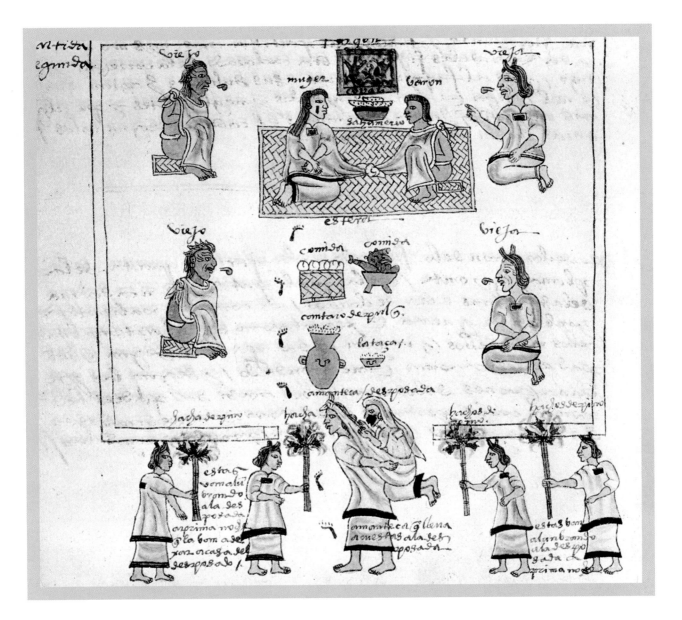

School Life

At about age ten, Aztec children went to school. There were separate schools for boys and girls. Most commoners attended a *telpochcalli,* or youth house. The telpochcalli was located at the temple for the calpulli. Students learned history, religion, public speaking, singing, and dancing. Music and dance were an important part of religious

This page from the sixteenth-century Codex Mendoza depicts an Aztec wedding.

ceremonies, and everyone was expected to take part. Boys also received military training and learned the skills necessary to construct public buildings. Girls learned the activities they would perform at various religious ceremonies.

Noble children, and some commoners who showed special skill or intelligence, went to a *calmecac*. Each town or city had one of these schools for boys and one for girls. Here, students learned the skills they would need to be government officials, priests, and military officers. Students lived in the calmecacs and had to follow strict regulations. They awoke before sunrise and bathed in cold water. Religious instruction was more intense than in a telpoch-calli, and at times students had to go without food and cut themselves to offer their blood to the gods.

Calmecac students learned history, math, astronomy, and law and received musical instruction. Students studied the paintings that appeared in codices, or books of manuscript pages held together by

This piece of carved stone was once part of a calmacec.

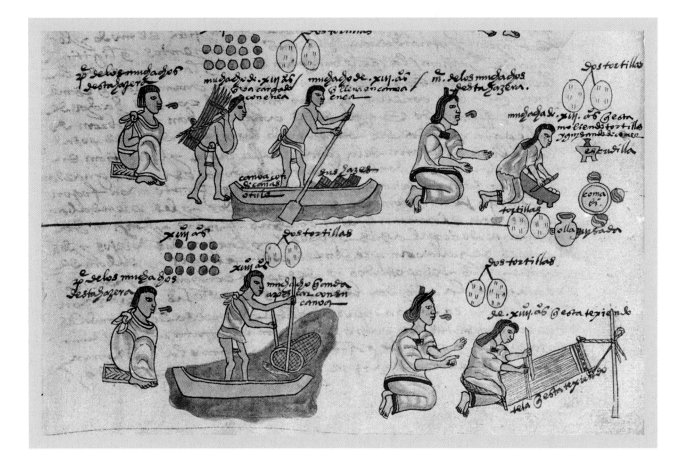

stitching. They were expected to learn and memorize the teachings they received verbally. Poetry was passed from one generation to the next in this way. Aztec poems told about the people's history as well as raising questions about the meaning of life and death.

In their late teens, Aztec youth began to think about marriage. Their parents helped them find a husband or wife, using someone who specialized in arranging marriages. The entire wedding ceremony lasted several days and included feasts, music, and speeches made by elderly relatives. The speeches were a kind of education, as they instructed the couple on how to be good mates and parents. Pipiltin men could have more than one wife. One wife usually had higher social rank than the others, and her children shared her rank.

This codex page depicts Aztec parents teaching their children how to perform various common tasks.

CHAPTER FIVE

A WORLD SHAPED BY RELIGIOUS IDEAS

T he prisoner lay stretched out on his back, his chest bare. Several priests held him to the stone surface, while another priest held a knife. Made of stone, the knife's tip was sharpened to a fine point. With a swift motion, the priest stabbed the prisoner's chest, made a cut, and then removed his still-beating heart. The heart and blood were offered to the gods, to thank them for all they had done for the Aztecs.

Most historians agree that human sacrifice was part of Aztec religion. Humans had sacrificed each other in Mesoamerica for thousands of years before the Mexica reached the Valley of Mexico. The earlier peoples sometimes also practiced **ritual cannibalism** as a small part of their religion, and the Aztecs did as well. These practices might seem cruel today, but they made sense to the Mesoamericans.

The killings were just one part of the many different rites and ceremonies that defined the Aztecs' religion. Food was offered to

the gods, and sweet-smelling substances called incense were burned. The Aztecs believed many things found in the world should be given back to the gods as thanks or to win their favor. Human blood was simply one of those things.

This sixteenth-century Spanish illustration depicts Aztecs performing a human sacrifice.

CREATION OF THE UNIVERSE

To the Aztecs, their world was not the only one that ever existed. They believed they lived during a period known as the Fifth Sun, which followed four other worlds that had been destroyed. Before the creation of the five suns of existence, an energy, or

ritual cannibalism (RICH-oo-uhl KAN-uh-buhl-izm) eating human flesh as part of a religious ceremony

The Past Is Present
THE HEALING POWER OF NATURE

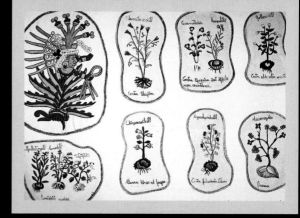

Aztec physicians turned to the natural world to find remedies for the ailments that affected the Aztec people. Many physicians were skilled herbalists who specialized in the use of plant life to treat illness. Much of what we know about their practices comes from the *Badianus Manuscript*, an

illustrated text written in 1552 by two Aztec natives. The book reveals that Aztec physicians used about two hundred plants and trees to treat illness. Many of their cures have been proven to be effective by modern scientific research. A painkiller called *chicalote* was a plant similar to the opium poppy, which was used in Western and Eastern medicine for many years. The sap of the agave plant was used to clean wounds and has since been shown to kill deadly bacteria. Herbs are still used in modern medicine, including aloe to treat skin ailments, lemon to treat coughs and sore throats, and ginger to relieve nausea.

force, filled the universe. The Aztecs believed this force had two parts, which they saw as being male and female. This cosmic couple had four sons. Each was associated with one of the directions on a compass: east, west, north, and south.

Sacrifices were an important part of the Aztec religion.

The Aztecs believed the universe had three distinct parts. At the top was heaven, which had up to thirteen different layers and was the home of the gods. Next came the world of human existence. Below that was an underworld, also with different layers. When people died, their souls went to the underworld.

After the destruction of the Fourth Sun, the gods met around a fire to discuss creating another world. One of the gods, Nanahuatzin, threw himself into the fire and was transformed into the sun. A second god followed him and became the moon. The god Quetzalcoatl then

Sacrifices were an important part of the Aztec religion.

created humans, by mixing some of his own blood with the ground bones of dead humans of the past. The Aztecs' myths say that their gods sacrificed all or part of themselves to create something new, including human life. Sacrifice was an important part of life, and the Aztecs believed they had to repay the gods with the different sacrifices they made.

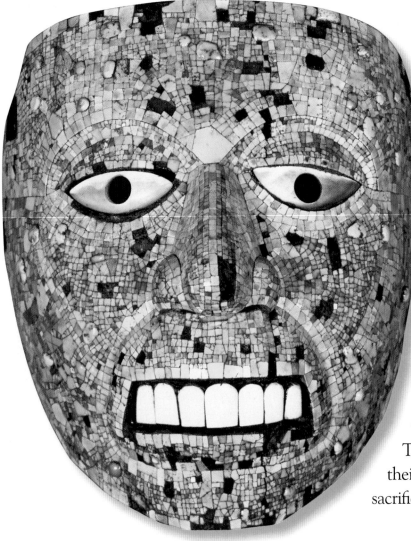

This Aztec mask is meant to represent the face of Quetzalcoatl.

MAJOR GODS

In daily life, the Aztecs worshipped a number of gods and goddesses—as many as two hundred, according to some historians. The Aztecs also believed in a spiritual force, called *teotl*, which filled parts of nature and even some humans, such as a tlatoani. A tree, a rainstorm, and even a cave could have teotl and play a role in shaping human life.

The god most closely associated with the Mexica is Huitzilopochtli, the warrior god who led them to Tenochtitlan. The Aztecs associated him with their ancestors and with war and sacrifice. Tezcatlipoca was a powerful

The Aztecs worshipped the deity Tlatecuhtli.

and feared god. He could see everything that happened in the human world and could predict events. Given his great powers, he was associated with the Aztec kings. Goddesses, such as Tonantzin, were often tied to forces that promoted life and childbirth. Chalchiuhtlicue was the goddess of running water, lakes, and the sea.

Good crop production was a major part of life, and gods tied to agriculture were especially important. The Aztecs borrowed their rain god, Tlaloc, from earlier Mesoamerican people. Giving thanks to him was thought to guarantee the rains would come each spring. Making him an important god also helped the Aztecs in their political effort to show their ties to the Toltecs and other great civilizations before them.

SACRIFICES TO THE GODS

In some ways, the things that the Aztecs offered to their gods were like the tribute the Aztecs expected from defeated enemies. The Aztecs hoped the sacrifices would keep the gods happy so they would provide them with good crops and make their lives easy. Human sacrifice, however, was the most powerful gift the

This statue of Chalchiuhtlicue dates to sometime between 1300 and 1500 CE.

Aztecs could offer their gods. In addition to removing a beating heart, the Aztecs and other Mesoamericans killed their victims in other ways. These included beheading, drowning, and burning.

Human sacrifices let people imitate the gods. The gods, traditionally, had been both creators and destroyers. By killing a prisoner or other sacrifice victim, the Aztecs were acting as destroyers. But the offering of blood to the gods was meant to give the gods life and ensure new life on Earth. The gods, the Aztecs believed, needed blood to survive. After some sacrifices, the bodies of the victims were cut up and parts of them were eaten. This too, the Aztecs thought, was for their gods. Even though humans ate the flesh, the people believed the gods received energy from it.

Most sacrifice victims were treated well before their deaths. The Aztecs saw them as human representatives of the gods they would be offered to. The victims were housed and fed, sometimes for months. Sacrifice victims for certain gods, such as Tezcatlipoca, were fed and clothed as if they were nobles. Both the Aztecs and the peoples they defeated believed that being sacrificed was honorable, although individual victims might still resist their fate. Women and children were sometimes sacrificed. Given the honor of being a victim, some people willingly chose to give their lives to the gods.

Human sacrifice also had a political role. The public killings demonstrated the vast power of the government over the people and made defeated enemies fearful. Seeking victims was one reason for Aztec warfare. In fact, the people of Mesoamerica seemed to have fought some battles just for this purpose. The Aztecs called these "flower wars," as soldiers were said to fall down dead as if they were cut flowers.

Keeping Track of Time

The Aztecs held religious ceremonies frequently. They used two calendars to help them keep track of the days when certain gods should be honored: the sacred calendar and the solar calendar.

The sacred calendar, by which fortunes were told, was 260 days long. This is about nine months, or a normal human pregnancy, probably the original basis for the calendar. In many parts of ancient Mexico, the count of 260 days was also important in organizing the agricultural year, playing a role in when farmers planted and harvested their crops.

The Aztec version of this calendar had 20 different name days, such as eagle, jaguar, house, water, and flower, which were taken from the natural world and everyday life. (Twenty units were also the basis of the Aztecs' counting system, perhaps because people have 10 fingers and 10 toes.) Each name day appeared with a number from 1 to 13, so one day might be called 4 Jaguar. Twenty day names and 13 numbers—20 times 13—equals 260 days. The year was divided into what we call months. Each day of the month was associated with a particular religious ritual.

The calendar of days was recorded in a special book called a *tonalamatl*. Specially trained Aztec priests were thought to be able to look at the book, along with the weather and other elements of the environment, and make predictions. The priests would say if a certain day was good or bad for doing something, such as going to war. Parents who had children born on what was considered a bad day would wait for a good day to name the child.

The Calendar of Years

The second Aztec calendar is the solar year calendar of 365

ce tec patl. ques vnà piedra. de pedernal, a figura de hierro cõ que ellos sa crificaua? / ome quia vitl q̃ quere dezir. dos llo vezinas. o aqua ceros, / yei suchitl. que quiere dezir tres Rosas. / nau ci pac tl. que es. Vna cosa bib q̃ anda en el aqi como. ser pezilla

days. It was based on the movement of the sun around Earth, as modern calendars are. The year on this calendar was divided into 18 months of 20 days each. Each month was dedicated to a god or goddess, and a festival was held in his or her honor. The Aztecs started the year in what is now February, and the sacrifices held then were meant to bring rains later in the year.

With 18 months of 20 days each, the Aztecs had five days left at the end of the 365-day year. Every fourth year, there was a sixth day, just as February has an extra day in leap years. This period

This page from the Codex Borbonicus *depicts the creation of the Aztec calendar.*

before the new year was called *nemontemi*. The Aztecs considered them unlucky days. People tried to do as little as possible during nemontemi, so they could lower their chances of having something bad happen. It was believed that children born during this time would lead unlucky lives.

As with the days on the 260-day cycle, the years counted on the solar calendar had names taken from nature and everyday life. There were four year names: reed, rabbit, house, and flint knife. They too were paired with the numbers 1 through 13. The names and numbers were matched up to create a 52-year cycle, similar to what is called a century today. The Aztecs believed that the end of the Fifth Sun would come at the completion of a 52-year cycle. When one of those cycles ended, people put out all their fires and threw away their common household items. Then they waited to see if the sun would rise to start the next cycle.

Meanwhile, priests scanned the skies for the Pleiades, one of the groups of stars nearest Earth. Seeing the stars meant the world would not end. The priests

The famous Aztec sun stone was once thought to be a representation of the Aztec calendar.

conquistador (kahn-KEES-tuh-dohr) soldier sent to seize foreign lands for Spain

then held a sacrifice and started a fire that would be used to start new fires across the empire. The day after this New Fire ceremony, people bought new items for their homes.

ARCHITECTURE AND ART

Aztec architecture had a practical purpose, but it also showed the skills of the engineers or architects who designed the buildings. Working with stone, the Aztecs constructed their most impressive buildings in Tenochtitlan. The Spanish **conquistador** Bernal Díaz del Castillo described the structures he saw, writing, "the great towers . . . and buildings rising from the water . . . some of our soldiers even asked whether the things that we saw were not a dream."

In the heart of the city was the Templo Mayor, which was surrounded by other sacred sites and buildings used by priests, including schools and a ball court. The main temple pyramid was the largest building in the city. Its great height was supposed to suggest the hill where the god Huitzilopochtli was born. Temples in general represented mountains, which the Aztecs saw as sources of water and the home of their ancestors.

Handsome artwork and handwriting appeared in codices, often recording historical events or religious rites. The Aztecs are also considered master sculptors. Other Mesoamericans sculpted, but the Aztecs' styles of sculpture found in Tenochtitlan were copied across the empire. Most statues and stone carvings had religious meaning, and Aztecs frequently placed large stone statues within their temples. People often kept small images of the gods in their homes.

Carved female figures were often shown kneeling, and males were shown sitting. Artists attempted to capture the beauty of women and the strength of men in their sculptures. Many surviving sculptures of animals, such as jaguars, have been found. A flea was also the subject of one Aztec sculpture. Painting was less common. The paintings that remain are murals found on the inside walls of several buildings.

Priests set huge fires at temples during New Fire ceremonies.

Detailed ceramic vases have been found at the site of Tenochtitlan.

This necklace was buried in an Aztec royal tomb.

CRAFT TURNED INTO ART

Ceramics, jewelry, and feather work often rose to the level of great art. Although most pottery was meant to be used in the kitchen, some had very colorful designs. Aztec potters did not use a wheel, as most modern potters do. Instead, the Aztecs built up their pieces by adding separate strands of clay. Feather workers also had great skill. To create an animal or another detailed image, they first drew an outline of the design on paper or cotton. They then glued on different colored feathers.

The Aztecs also valued jewelry of gold and silver. Items that survived to the present include detailed images of human faces and animals. Jade, a blue-green gemstone, was highly prized and was worn only by royalty. Masks made of jade still exist today. Turquoise, obsidian, and wood were also used to make masks, and some were covered with different colored tiles. Masks represented the gods and could be used as decorations or worn during certain rituals.

CHAPTER SIX

AN EMPIRE ENDS—AND LIVES ON

Montezuma II led the Aztecs at the time the Spanish arrived in what is now Mexico.

In his palace, Montezuma II heard disturbing news. A report reached Tenochtitlan from the east: strange "mountains" were seen floating on the water. They reached the shore in what is now Yucatan, Mexico, and strange-looking beings came out of them. These newcomers had beards and much shorter hair than the Aztecs wore. Before these men arrived, Montezuma and his highest priests had heard of other odd events happening in the empire.

Were those events omens that something terrible would happen to the Aztecs?

The "mountains" that reached Yucatan were actually large ships, sailing from the Spanish colony of Cuba. They arrived in Mexico in 1517, carrying conquistadores seeking riches. Another vessel arrived the next year, and the Spaniards on board headed farther west. In 1518, they met representatives sent by Montezuma. This meeting marked the first direct contact between the Aztec and Spanish empires—a meeting that would seem to prove that the omens were right.

FIRST CONTACT—AND CONFLICT

The men Montezuma sent to greet the Spaniards wore fine cotton clothing and gold jewelry. They traded some of their gold for glass beads and offered the strangers food. After receiving the beads, the emperor made plans to defend his lands, in case the Spaniards returned and intended to attack.

Hernán Cortés led the conquistadores that landed in the Yucatan.

This sixteenth-century illustration depicts Malintzin speaking to Cortés.

The Spaniards did return, in 1519. About five hundred men under the command of Hernán Cortés came ashore on the island of Cozumel, where they met a shipwrecked sailor who knew the local language. The Spanish continued inland and traded gifts with a local tribe. One gift Cortés received was a slave named Malintzin. The Spanish called her Malinche. She spoke both Nahuatl and Aztec. She and the shipwrecked sailor served as Cortés's translators. The conquistadores moved on.

Hearing of the arrival of a larger group of Spaniards, Montezuma once again chose not to fight the invaders. Historians have debated why the emperor did not attack. In early years, some said Montezuma thought Cortés was the god Quetzalcoatl returned to Earth. More recently, some experts say the tlatoani did not think this but that he did associate the Spaniards with historical and religious forces that made the strangers worthy of respect—and curiosity. Furthermore, he did not think the foreigners were a threat: warfare in the Aztec world was always announced beforehand.

The Past Is Present
SWEET TREATS

E ven the most enthusiastic chocolate lovers may not know that the history of this treat begins in Mesoamerica. Chocolate is made from cacao beans, which grow on trees. The word *chocolate* probably comes from the Nahuatl word meaning "bitter water." The Aztecs used the beans to make a chocolate drink. The best drink was called either *cacahuatl* or *xocolatl* and was only drunk by the nobles or warriors. The first European contact with chocolate came when the Spaniards invaded the Aztec homeland. Within a few years, the Spaniards enslaved native peoples to harvest cacao. It was shipped back to Spain

and eventually became a favorite treat throughout Europe. Today, the average American eats about 12 pounds (5.4 kilograms) of chocolate a year, a small amount compared to Austria's average of 20 pounds (9 kg) and Switzerland's 23 pounds (10.4 kg). Worldwide sales of chocolate are more than US$50 billion annually!

As depicted in this nineteenth-century illustration, Cortés was aided by the Tlaxcalans in his attack on Tenochtitlan.

Montezuma sent more gifts to the conquistadores, including a large gold disk that represented the sun. Seeing the Aztecs' great wealth, Cortés marched on Tenochtitlan. He had already won over native allies who resented paying tribute to the Triple Alliance. The Spaniards would gain more help as they headed west. Most important of all was the support of Tlaxcala, the home of the Aztecs' longtime enemy.

At first, the Tlaxcalans resisted the invaders, thinking they were allies of Montezuma. Several thousand attacked the Spanish, who fought back with their superior weapons: powerful crossbows, small cannons, firearms called arquebuses, and long spears. The Spanish had another advantage—their horses. Ancient relatives of horses had once roamed North America, but they had died out long before the Aztecs rose to power. The Aztecs called the Spanish horses "deer," and were amazed by their size and strength. From high atop their horses, Spanish soldiers could charge enemy warriors on foot and swing their swords at them from a great height.

After several battles, the leaders of Tlaxcala agreed to Cortés's call for peace. The Tlaxcala and their allies would now help the Spaniards, and the conquistadores would use the altepetl as a base. Peace came just in time for the Spaniards. As the conquistador Bernal Díaz del Castillo later wrote, "We were already lean and worn out and discontented with the war."

Montezuma Meets Cortés

Montezuma heard about the Spanish alliance with Tlaxcala. He made plans to trick them before they could reach Tenochtitlan. The emperor convinced the allied city of Cholula to invite the Spaniards in as guests. Once inside the city, the Cholulans would ambush the Spaniards. A spy, however, told Cortés the Aztec plan, and his forces captured and killed the Cholulans leaders before they could attack. Montezuma then decided to let the Spaniards enter Tenochtitlan, where he might be able to launch a more successful ambush. By now, Montezuma surely knew the Spaniards were mere humans, as they had refused the blood and flesh his diplomats offered them. Real gods, the Aztecs thought, would have accepted the sacrifices.

Cortés and his men easily defeated the Cholulans.

On November 8, 1519, the emperor and the conquistador finally met. Cortés rode his horse along one of the causeways linking Tenochtitlan to the mainland. Montezuma came to greet him. They exchanged gifts and pleasant words. Later, they met in the emperor's palace. But the friendly first meeting did not ensure that the two sides would get along. Cortés wanted the Aztec Empire's vast wealth for Spain. He also wanted to make the native people Christians.

For about two weeks, the emperor treated the strangers as honored guests. But Cortés began to sense that at some point the Aztecs would trick him and attack his men. Before they did, however, the Spanish struck. Cortés had Montezuma kidnapped and held him prisoner in another palace. Over the next several months, Montezuma gave the Spaniards some of his great wealth and promised to obey King Charles V of Spain. Although a prisoner, the emperor still had contact with his advisers and tried to rule the best he could.

Montezuma and Cortés met peacefully on November 8, 1519.

Cortés soon wanted to destroy the Aztec religious statues in the Templo Mayor and end human sacrifice. Montezuma convinced him not to destroy the statues, but Cortés ordered the end to the sacrifices and put up a Christian cross in the Aztec temple. The Aztec priests and the people were angered by this attack on their faith. Some Aztec lords, who were military commanders, made plans to attack, and Montezuma told Cortés he should leave the city before he was killed.

The Battles for an Empire

Cortés left the city with some of his men and went to meet other Spaniards who had arrived in the eastern city of Veracruz. Meanwhile, the Spanish troops in Tenochtitlan faced new challenges. The Aztecs disobeyed an order to not carry out human sacrifices during an important festival for the god Tezcatlipoca. The Spaniards learned that the Aztecs planned to rebel after the ceremony, and struck first. A document of the time describes how the Spaniards stormed the temple and "attacked all the celebrants, stabbing them, spearing them, striking them with their swords." Several thousand Aztecs died during the slaughter.

When Cortés returned in June 1520, the Spaniards and their Mexica allies were back in the palace where Montezuma was imprisoned. Soon, the Aztecs launched a major attack, sending waves of warriors upon the palace. Others fired arrows and darts from the roofs of surrounding buildings. Montezuma went to the roof of the palace and ordered the warriors to stop. This time, the warriors who once obeyed his command battered him with stones and fired arrows at him. The former emperor fell, struck his head, and soon died. Cortés claimed he died from the head injury, but the Aztecs said the Spaniards killed him.

Cortés now prepared to leave Tenochtitlan. On the night of June 30, his men tried to sneak out of the city, taking with them several tons of gold and other valuables. Spotting them on the causeway, the Aztecs launched a fierce attack, killing several thousand Spaniards and their allies, and taking many prisoners. The Spanish referred to this as *La Noche Triste*, or "The Night of Sorrows."

Cortés and the other survivors circled north around the five lakes of the Valley of Mexico, heading for safety in Tlaxcala. There, he would plan his final attack on the Mexica. In early July, an Aztec force attacked the Spaniards at Otumba. Although outnumbered, the Spanish cavalry was able to do heavy damage, and the Spaniards won the battle. Back in Tlaxcala, Cortés made plans to take control of the entire Aztec Empire.

The conquistadores may have killed Montezuma.

Cuitlahuac was the brother of Montezuma.

The Final Assault

Over the next few months, Cortés received weapons and supplies from Spain. Finally, in April 1521, about seven hundred Spaniards and tens of thousands of native allies began their assault on the Aztec capital.

By this time, Cortés was unintentionally using another weapon against the Aztecs: disease. The Spaniards had brought smallpox with them, and since the disease did not exist in the Americas, the local people had no natural defenses against it. The

Many Aztecs died of smallpox carried by the Spanish.

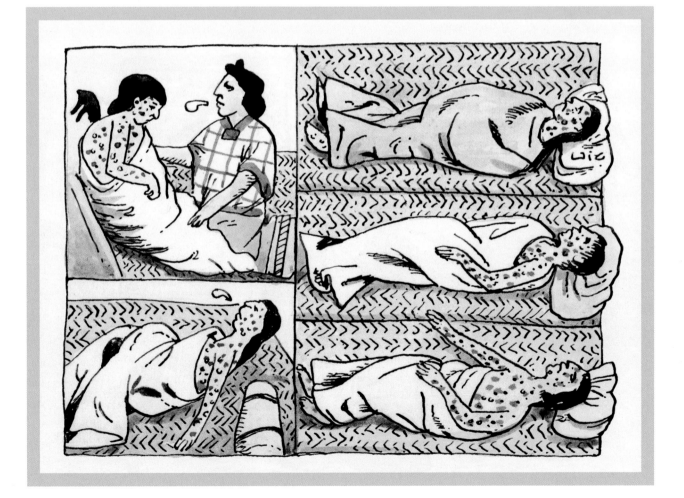

new emperor Cuitlahuac had died of the disease in December 1520, as had thousands of Aztecs. Still, when the Spaniards reached Tenochtitlan, they found a city prepared for war.

The Spanish attacked the city from two sides, along the causeways. The Aztecs fought from the rooftops. As the Spaniards conquered parts of the city, they destroyed all of the nearby buildings. The fighting, disease, and lack of food and water killed thousands of Aztec civilians. In August 1521, the new tlatoani, Cuauhtemoc, tried to flee the city by canoe but was captured. On August 13, Cuauhtemoc surrendered to Cortés. The great Aztec Empire was no more.

The Spanish destroyed many great works of art in their attempts to erase the Aztec religion.

LIFE AS A COLONY

Under Spanish rule, Tenochtitlan was renamed Mexico City. The Aztec lands and other areas around it were called New Spain. The colony became a major source of silver for the Spanish crown. Roman Catholic priests began to spread their religion and tried to wipe out all traces of the Aztec faith. In the capital, that meant building a huge new church on the grounds where the Templo Mayor and other religious buildings once stood. The defeated people, however, did not give up all traces of their old religion. In their art, they sometimes blended Christian images of Jesus Christ, Mary, and the cross with symbols from their old religion. This blending of Christian and Aztec images still continues today.

In some places, Spanish colonists owned large areas of land. Under a policy called *encomienda*, the landowners were in charge of the native people who farmed it for them. The owner was supposed to convert the Aztecs to Christianity and protect them from enemy attack. In return, the people paid the owners tribute. Under this system, some Aztecs faced harsh treatment.

This disk, dating to around 1540, contains a blend of Christian and Aztec imagery.

The Spanish counted on the help of Aztec nobles to rule the new colony. They let the nobles stay in power in cities and towns across the old empire. Members of the old royal family held important positions in Mexico City for decades. Over time, however, Spain sent more government officials to run the colony. They worked with local officials to make sure tributes were paid. A social and political order developed that put Spaniards at the top and natives at the bottom. In the middle were mestizos—children with one Spanish and one Aztec parent.

THE AZTEC INFLUENCE TODAY

It took New Spain three hundred years to win its independence from Spain and become the nation of Mexico. The Aztec influence lives on in the name Mexico, which comes from *Mexica*. Mexico's flag shows images relating to the legendary founding of Tenochtitlan. In the center of the flag is an eagle on a cactus, referring to the sign the god Huitzilopochtli told the Mexica to look for hundreds of years earlier.

To this day, some aspects of the Roman Catholic faith in Mexico have connections to the Aztecs. The Day of the Dead, celebrated at the end of October into November, recalls Aztec rites to honor the dead. Skeleton masks worn today sometimes look like the skulls seen in Aztec art. The Aztecs believed death was natural and not to be feared. The Mexican Day of the Dead ceremonies carry on that idea.

Parts of Aztec life live on in Mexico and other places around the world. Mexican meals include foods commonly eaten in Aztec times. The Aztecs also gave us the words for "avocado," "tomato," and "chocolate." Children who try to break piñatas at parties may be

Modern-day Mexico City stands upon the former site of Tenochtitlan.

imitating an old Aztec rite. Some Mexicans say this modern activity is based on an ancient one, when clay water pots dedicated to the rain god Tlaloc were raised and then broken with wooden sticks.

Nahuatl is still spoken by more than one million Mexicans, some of whom have never learned Spanish. Nahuatl names for cities and towns are still used, both within and outside Mexico City.

Mexican soccer star Cuauhtemoc Blanco (in green) was named after the last of the Aztec emperors.

Sports fans might know that the Mexican national soccer team plays in a stadium named for the Aztecs. A college in San Diego, California, calls its athletic teams the Aztecs. Some Mexicans give their children Aztec names, such as those of the emperors. Cuauhtemoc Blanco, one of Mexico's greatest soccer players, was named for the last Aztec emperor. The names of the emperors also appear on businesses and in geography. The word *calpulli* lives on as the name of a Mexican dance company based in New York City.

It's not surprising that links to Aztec culture are found in the Americas outside Mexico. Millions of Mexicans have migrated northward—back in the direction of the original Mexica homeland. Some scholars have even suggested that the Mexica came from what is now the southwestern United States. Nahuatl is part of a family of languages that includes ones spoken by Native American tribes in that part of the country.

While the original home of the Mexica is still a mystery, some Mexican Americans look to the Aztecs as a source of cultural pride. The movement began during the 1960s and remains alive today. Some Mexican Americans claim ties to Aztlan, the home of the Mexica before their migration. Mexican-born husband and wife painters Diego Rivera and Frida Kahlo were world-famous artists who often included Aztec themes in their art.

People of Mexican heritage have moved far beyond the Americas and settled throughout the world. They bring with them a culture tied to one of the world's great civilizations, the Aztecs. Although they could not survive contact with the Europeans, the Aztecs built—through conquest, trade, and diplomacy—a great empire with an enduring influence.

BIOGRAPHIES

ACAMAPICHTLI (REIGNED CA. 1375–1395) served as the first king of the Mexica after their arrival in Tenochtitlan.

AHUITZOTL (REIGNED 1486–1502) completed construction of the Templo Mayor and greatly extended the boundaries of the Aztec Empire. During his rule, the tlatoani of Tenochtitlan became the absolute leader of the Triple Alliance.

HERNÁN CORTÉS (1485–1547) led the invasion that ended Aztec rule and gave Spain control of central Mexico. He later claimed other lands for the Spanish crown.

CUAUHTEMOC (CA. 1495–1522) was the last Aztec emperor, ruling for less than one year. The Spanish killed him after they took control of the empire.

BERNAL DÍAZ DEL CASTILLO (CA. 1495–1584) fought under Hernán Cortés during the conquest of Mexico. Later, he wrote about his experiences, and his book remains an important primary source for historians.

ITZCOATL (REIGNED 1428–1440), tlatoani of Tenochtitlan, convinced the leaders of two other cities to unite and fight the Tepanecs. This was the beginning of the Triple Alliance, another name for the Aztec Empire.

MALINTZIN (CA. 1501–1550), also known as Malinche and Marina, was a slave who served as a translator for Hernán Cortés.

MONTEZUMA I (REIGNED 1440–1469) expanded the empire beyond the Valley of Mexico and made improvements to the Templo Mayor.

MONTEZUMA II (1466–1520) ruled as tlatoani with almost total control, more so than the emperors before him. He took control in 1502 and was in power when the Spanish first reached Tenochtitlan.

BERNARDINO DE SAHAGÚN (CA. 1500–1590) was a Roman Catholic priest who studied Nahuatl and wrote a dictionary of the language.

TEZOZOMOC (REIGNED CA. 1370–1426) was a leader of the Tepanecs and built a small empire before the rise of the Aztecs. He rewarded the Mexica for their service to him, allowing them to collect tribute.

TIZOC (REIGNED 1481–1486) was the seventh tlatoani of Tenochtitlan. His coronation war led to the loss of many Aztec troops, which his people saw as a bad omen.

TIMELINE

CA. 500 CE:
The city of Teotihuacan, whose culture influenced the Aztecs, reaches the height of its power.

CA. 1150:
The Toltecs begin moving into the Valley of Mexico.

1375:
Acamapichtli becomes the first tlatoani of the Mexica.

1200 **1300** **1400**

1325:
The Mexica found the city of Tenochtitlan on an island in Lake Texcoco.

CA. 1250—1300:
The Mexica reach the Valley of Mexico.

(timeline continued)

1486:
Ahuitzotl becomes tlatoani and asserts his power as head of the Triple Alliance. He greatly expands the empire.

CA. 1478:
The Aztecs lose a war to the Tarascans, who remain free from Aztec control.

1473:
Tenochtitlan defeats its neighboring city of Tlatelolco, home of the largest market in the Aztec Empire.

1425   **1450**   **1475**

1450:
A deadly famine begins and lasts for several years.

1440:
Montezuma I becomes tlatoani and begins to spread Aztec control beyond the Valley of Mexico.

1428:
Tenochtitlan, Texcoco, and Tlacopan form the Triple Alliance.

1427:
Itzcoatl unites the Mexica with the people of Texcoco and Tlacopan to fight the Tepanecs.

1521:
Cortés returns to Tenochtitlan with a massive army. The Spaniards defeat the Aztecs and take control of their empire.

1520:
Cortés leaves the city, and fighting breaks out between his remaining troops and the Aztecs. When Cortés returns, he and his men leave the city, though they suffer heavy losses along the way.

1519:
Hernán Cortés lands in Mexico and begins to head west toward Tenochtitlan. Along the way, the Spaniards fight the people of Tlaxcala and then convince them to become allies against the Aztecs. In November, Cortés and Montezuma meet. After several weeks, the Spaniards kidnap the emperor.

1500   **1525**

1518:
Representatives of Montezuma meet with another group of Spaniards.

1517:
Spanish conquistadores come ashore in eastern Mexico.

1502:
Montezuma II is chosen the next emperor.

GLOSSARY

artisans (AHR-ti-zuhnz) people who are skilled at working with their hands at a particular craft

conquistador (kahn-KEES-tuh-dohr) soldier sent to seize foreign lands for Spain

dike (DIKE) a high wall or dam that is built to hold back water and prevent flooding

domesticated (duh-MES-ti-kate-id) taken from the wild and tamed to be used by humans

dormant (DOR-muhnt) a volcano that is not doing anything now but could erupt again

drought (DROUT) a long period without rain

famines (FAM-inz) serious lack of food in a geographic area

hygiene (HYE-jeen) keeping yourself and the things around you clean, in order to stay healthy

loincloth (LOYN-klawth) garment worn around a man's waist

Mesoamerica (mez-oh-uh-MARE-ih-kuh) the area extending from central Mexico south to Honduras and Nicaragua in which pre-Columbian cultures thrived

migrate (MYE-grate) to move from one country or area to another

obsidian (uhb-SID-ee-uhn) a shiny, usually black glass created by volcanic activity

omen (OH-muhn) a sign or warning about the future

porters (POR-turz) people who carry equipment on an expedition or military mission

provinces (PRAH-vihn-sez) districts or regions of some countries

rite (RITE) a religious event or activity with special meaning

ritual cannibalism (RICH-oo-uhl KAN-uh-buhl-izm) eating human flesh as part of a religious ceremony

sacrificed (SAK-ruh-fised) killed as an offering to a god

sierra (see-ER-uh) a chain of hills or mountains with peaks that look like sharp, jagged teeth

subjects (SUHB-jekts) people who live under the authority of a king or a queen

tribute (TRIB-yoot) something done, given, or said to show thanks or respect, or to repay an obligation

tropical (TRAH-pi-kuhl) of or having to do with the hot, rainy areas close to the equator

FIND OUT MORE

BOOKS

Doeden, Matt. *The Aztecs: Life in Tenochtitlan*.
Minneapolis: Millbrook Press, 2010.

Ganeri, Anita. *How the Aztecs Lived*. New York: Gareth Stevens, 2011.

Green, Carl R. *Cortés: Conquering the Powerful Aztec Empire*.
Berkeley Heights, NJ: Enslow Publishers, 2010.

Kent, Deborah. *Mexico*. New York: Children's Press, 2010.

Somervill, Barbara A. *Empire of the Aztecs*.
New York: Chelsea House, 2010.

Visit this Scholastic Web site for more
information on Ancient Aztecs:
www.factsfornow.scholastic.com
Enter the keywords **Ancient Aztecs**

INDEX

Page numbers in *italics* indicate a photograph or map.

ABOUT THE AUTHOR

Michael Burgan is the author of more than 250 books for children and young adults, both fiction and non-fiction. His works include books on the Roman, Mongol, and Persian Empires and biographies of U.S. leaders. His graphic-novel adaptation of *Frankenstein* was a Junior Library Guild selection. A graduate of the University of Connecticut with a degree in history, Burgan is also a produced playwright. He lives in Santa Fe, New Mexico.